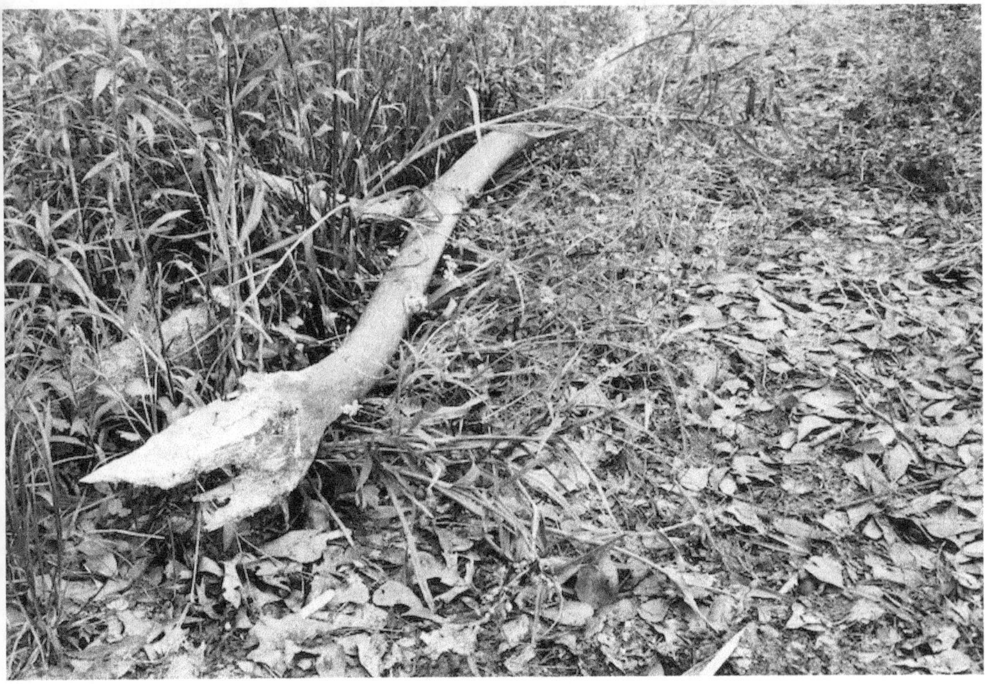

Broken and Astray
May 2015

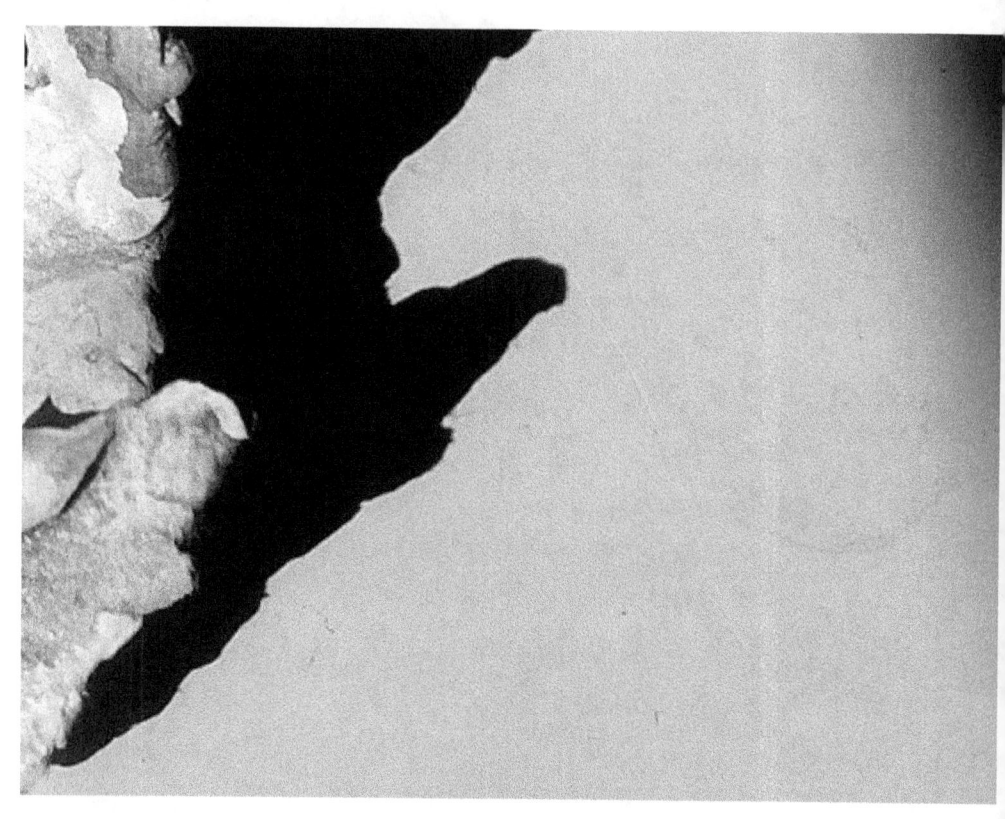

Fragment of a Dream
January 2016

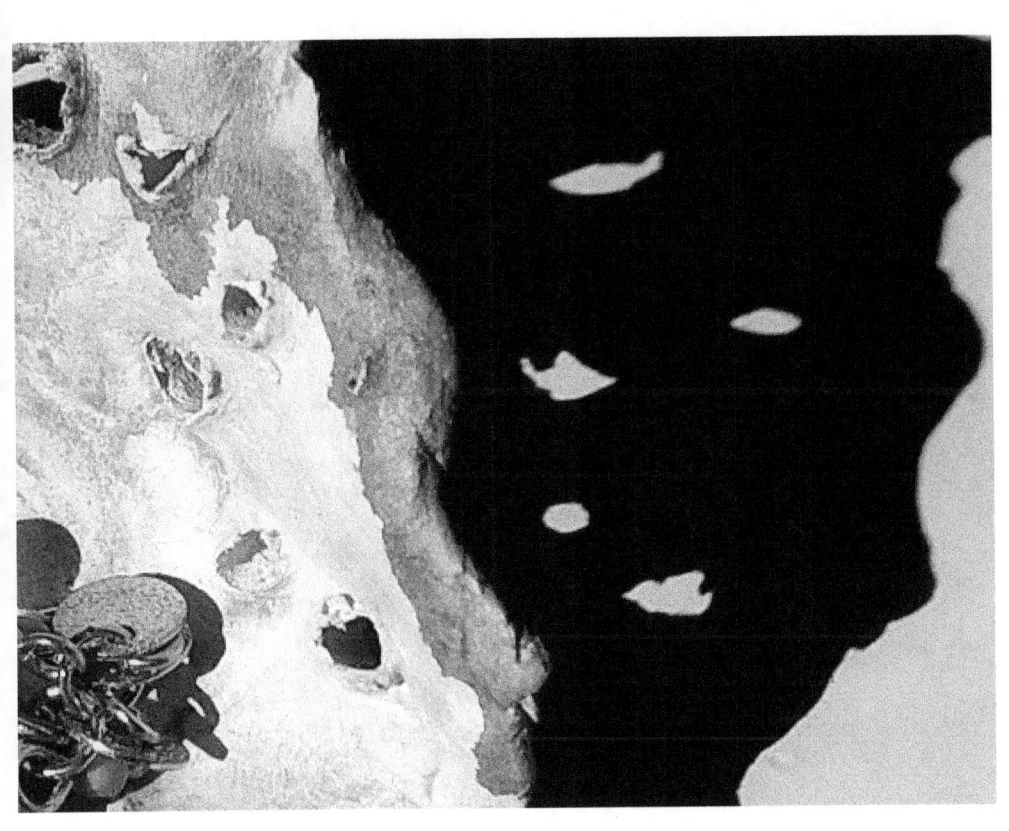

Fragment of a Wish
January 2016

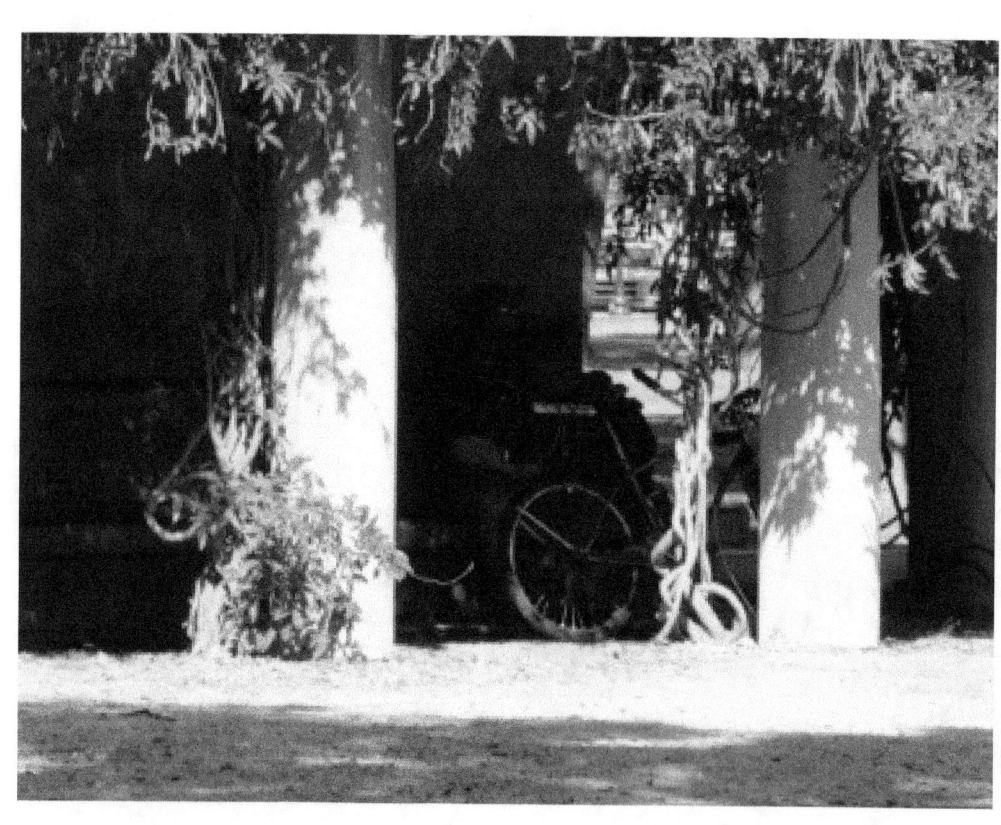

Unaware Traveler
April 2015

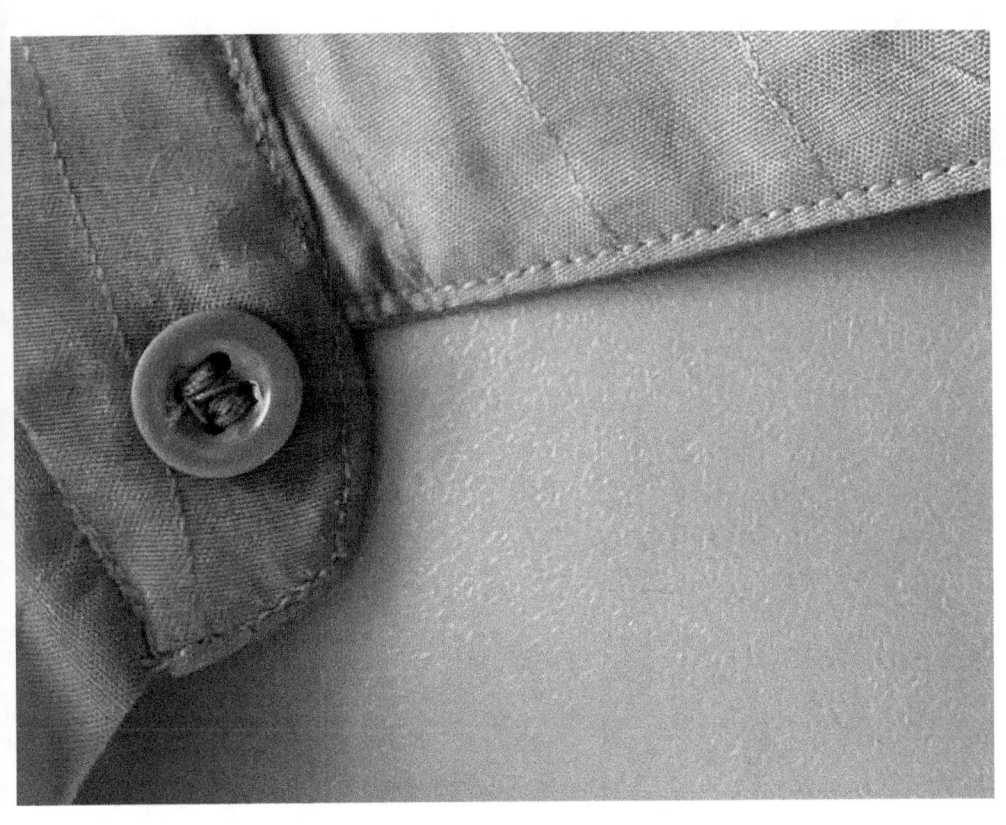

Forgotten Collar
July 2015

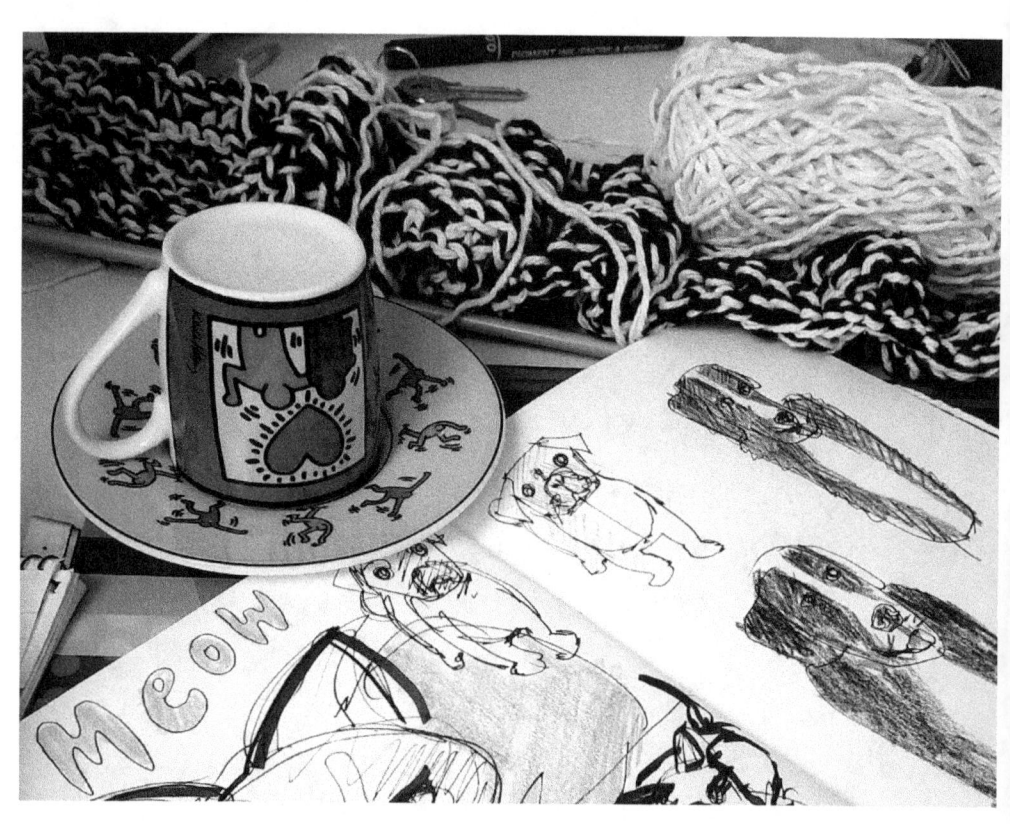

Forgotten or Abandoned Passions
July 2015

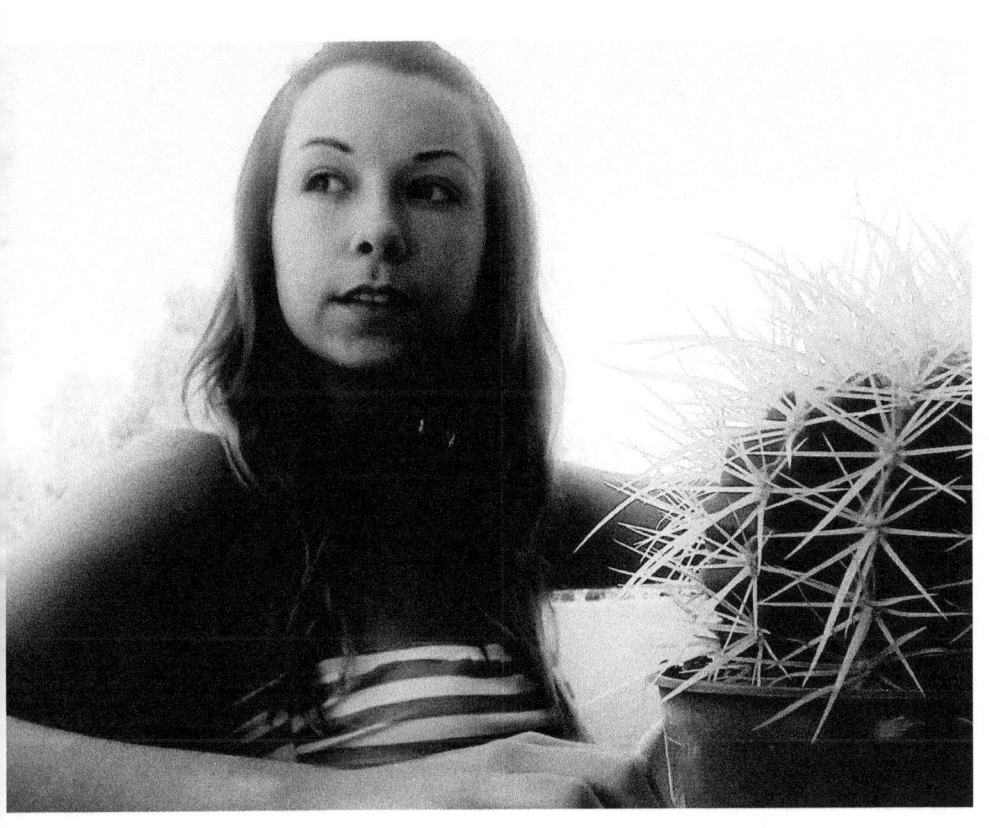

Self-Portrait with Cactus
June 2015

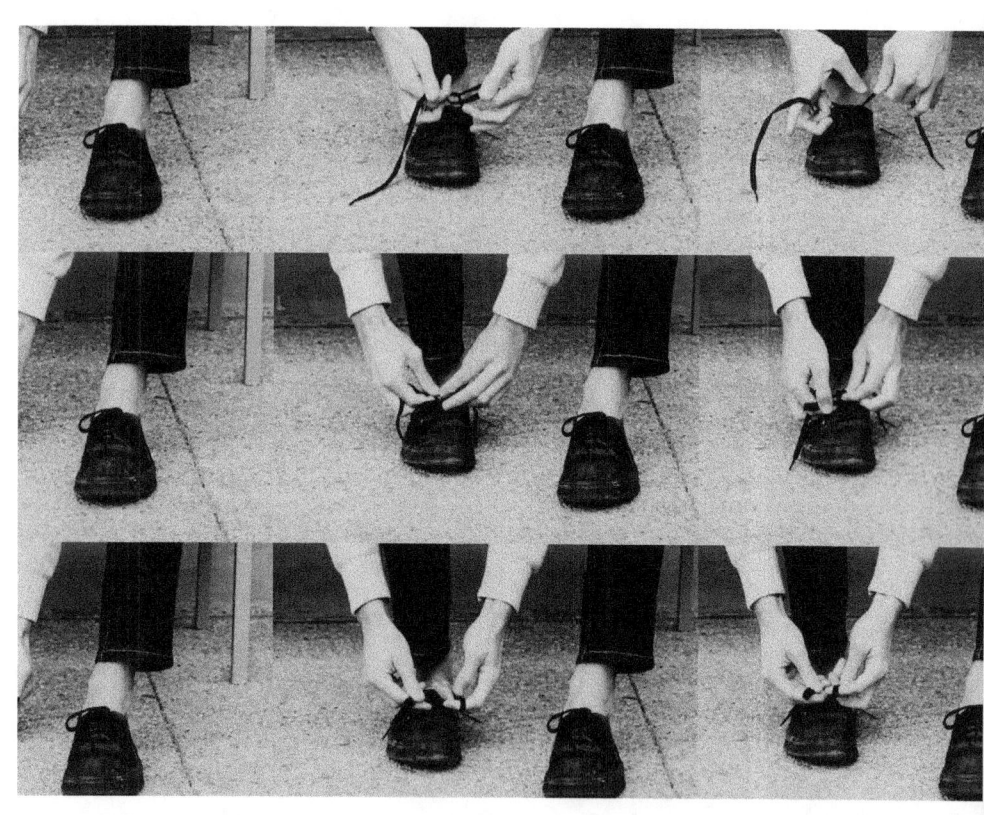

The Mundane
November 2014

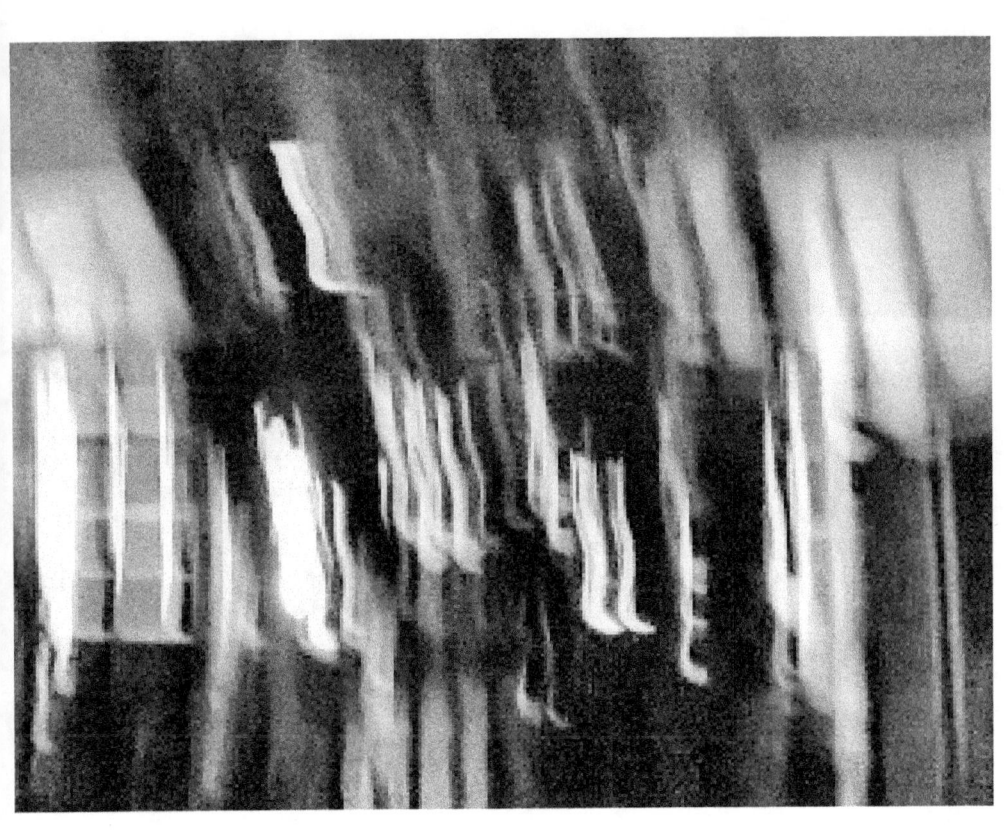

The Night's Impalpable Textures
December 2014

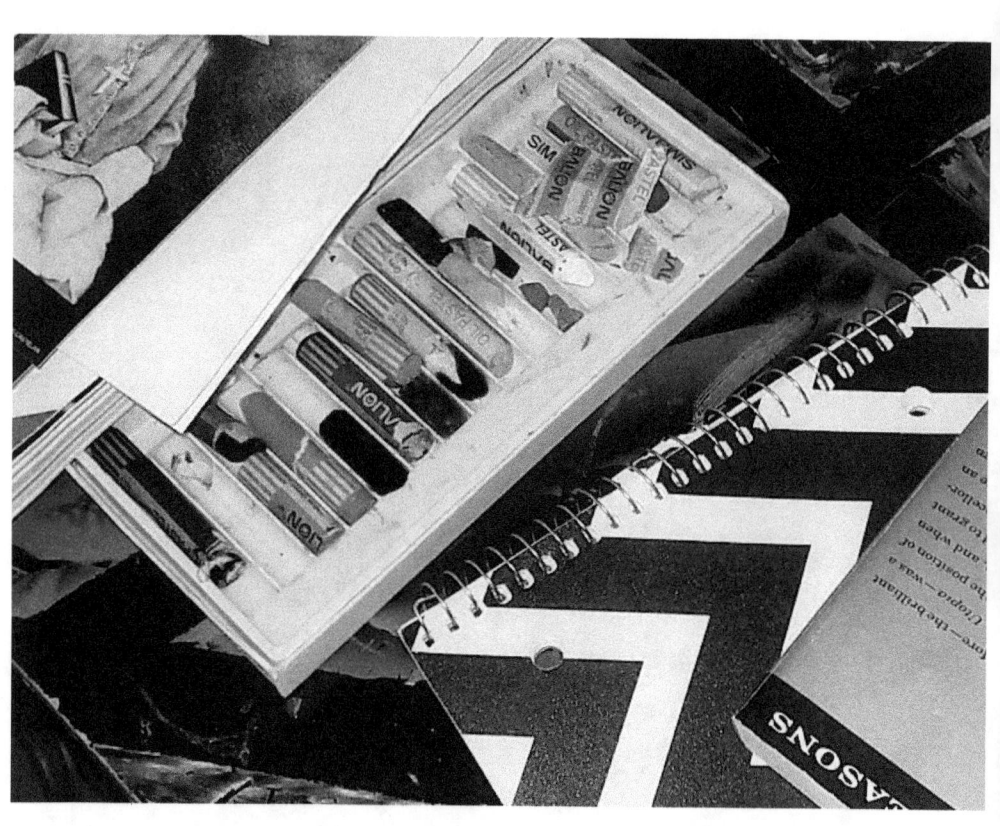

Restless Pursuits
May 2015

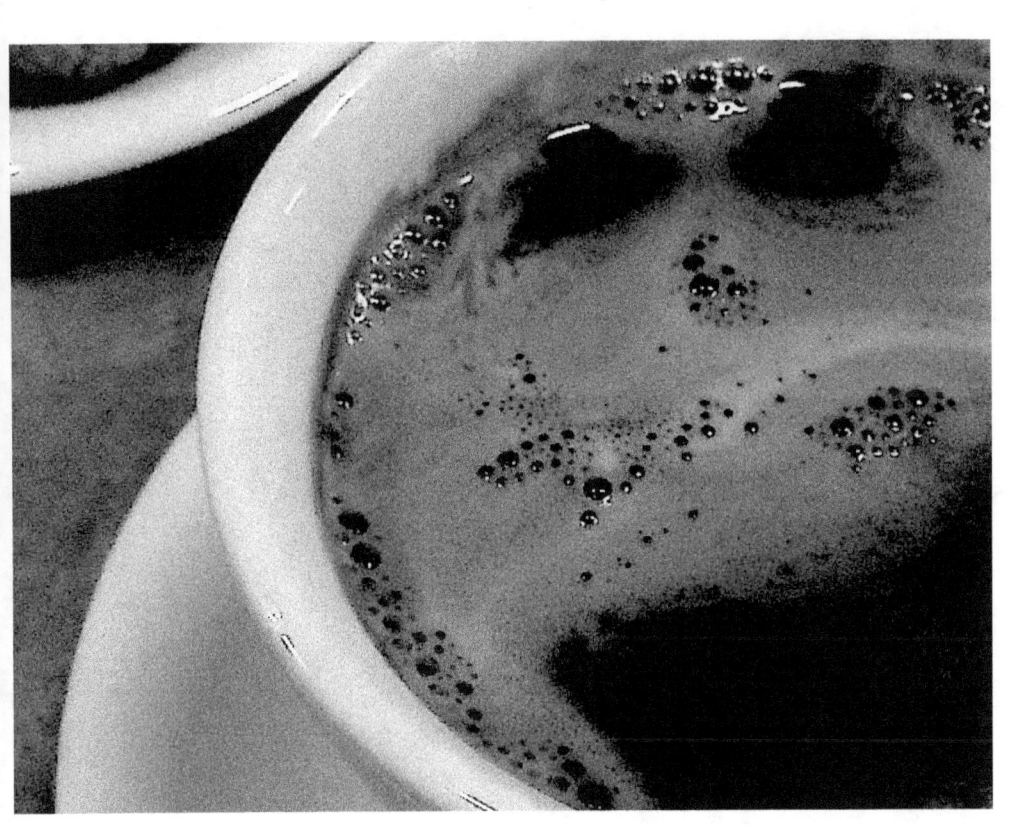

I Wish I Could Kiss the Barista
March 2015

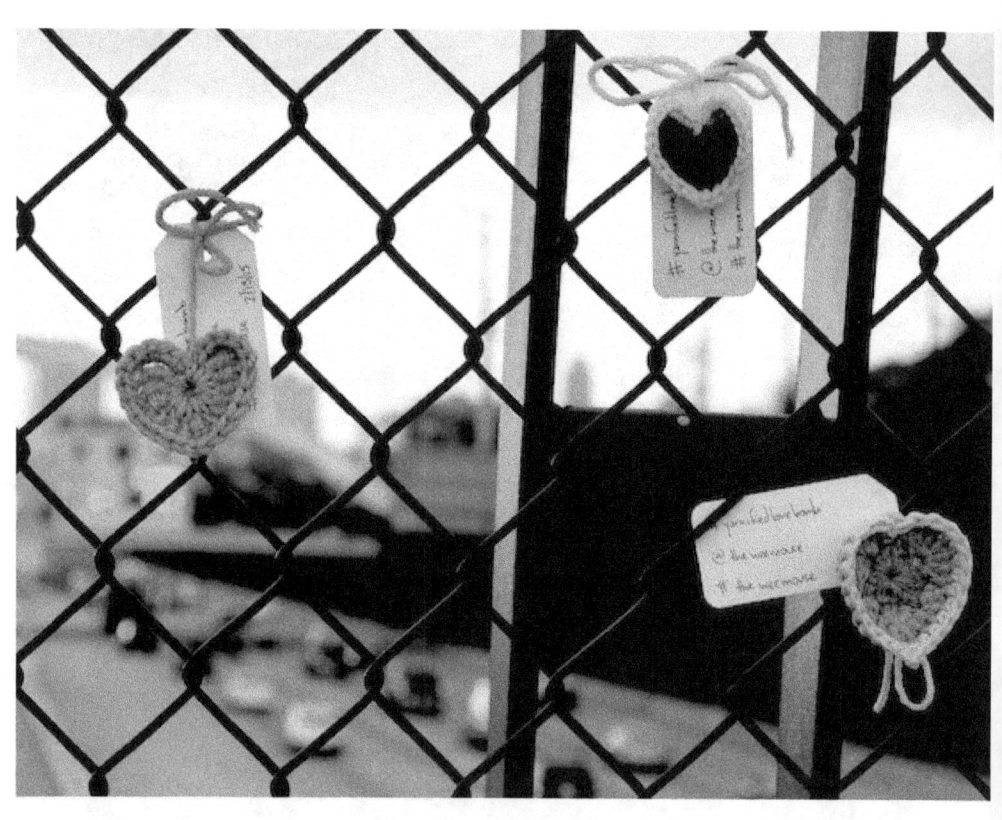

Yarn-Bombing the City with Brittany
May 2015

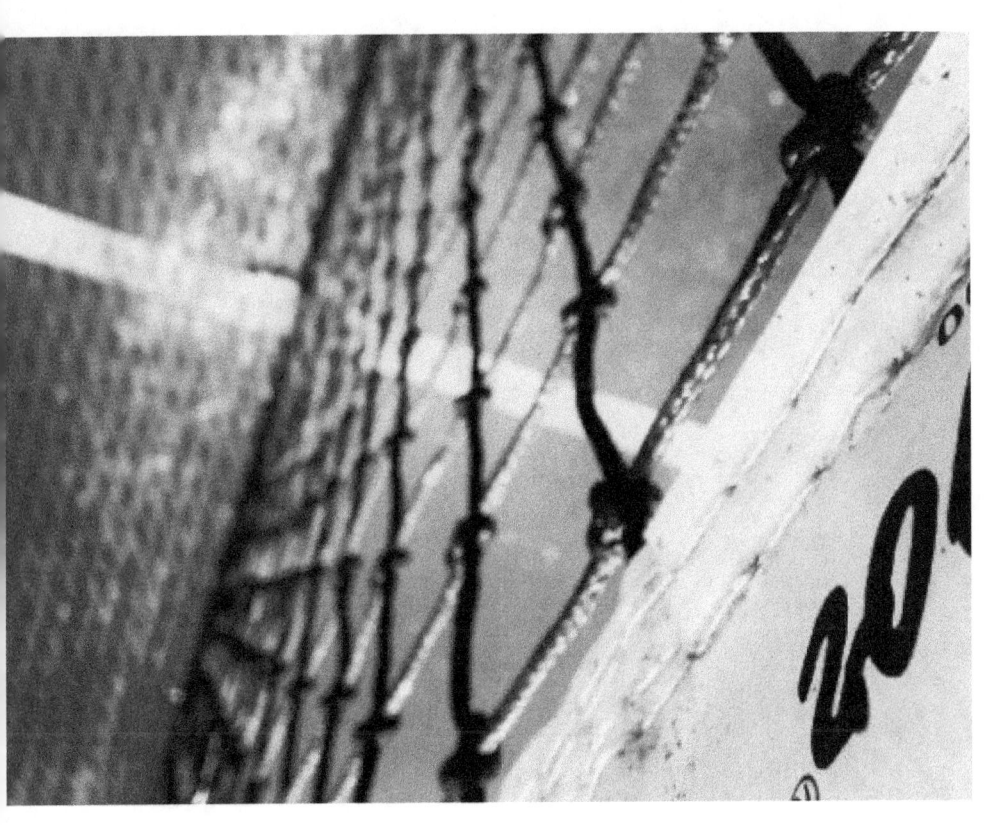

Aerial View of Net; Waugh Park
April 2015

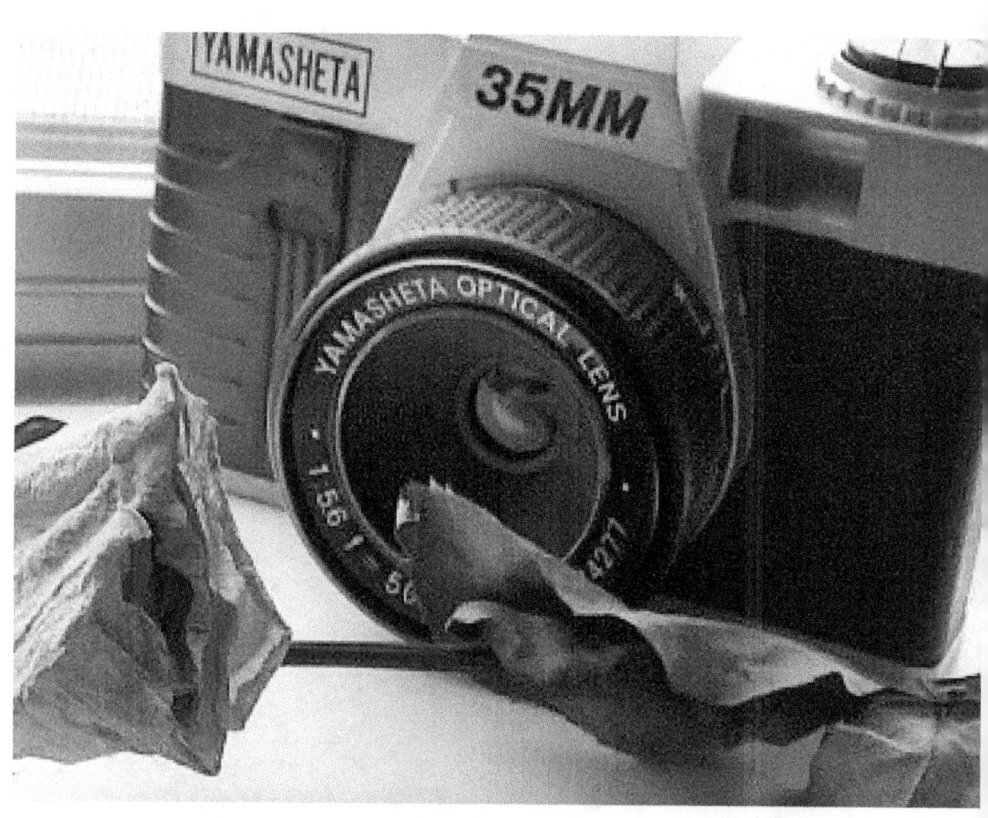

Whithering or Expired Memory
November 2014

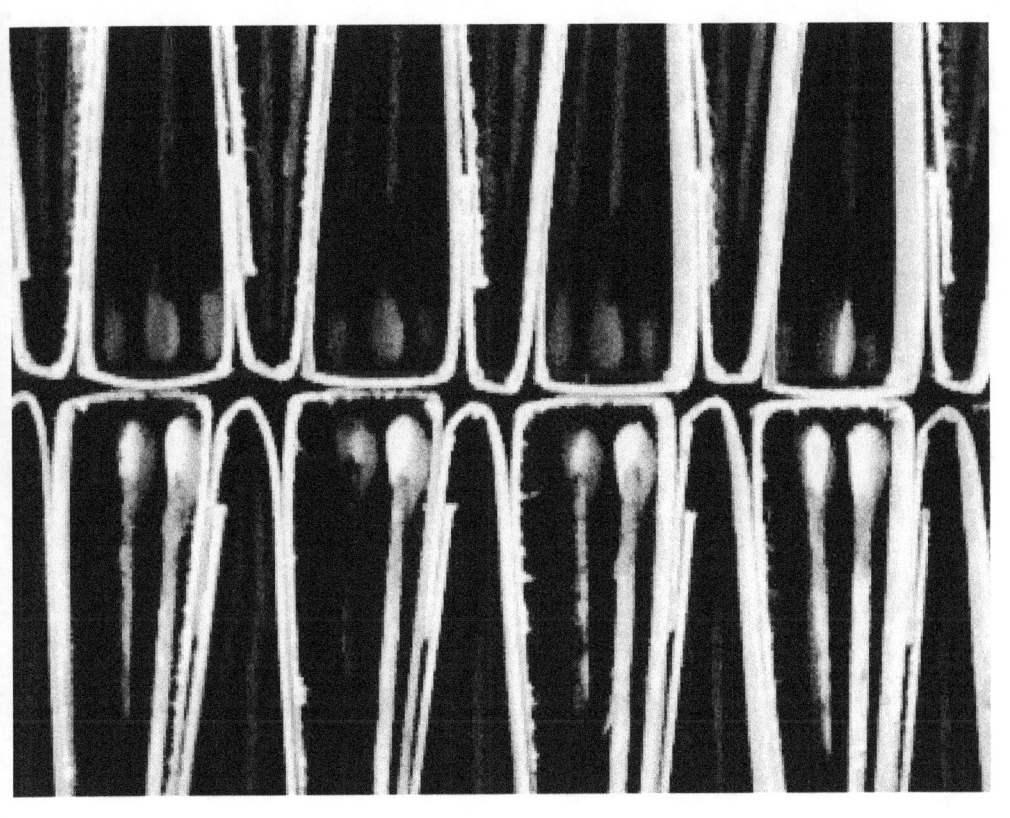

Matches for the Phoenix
December 2014

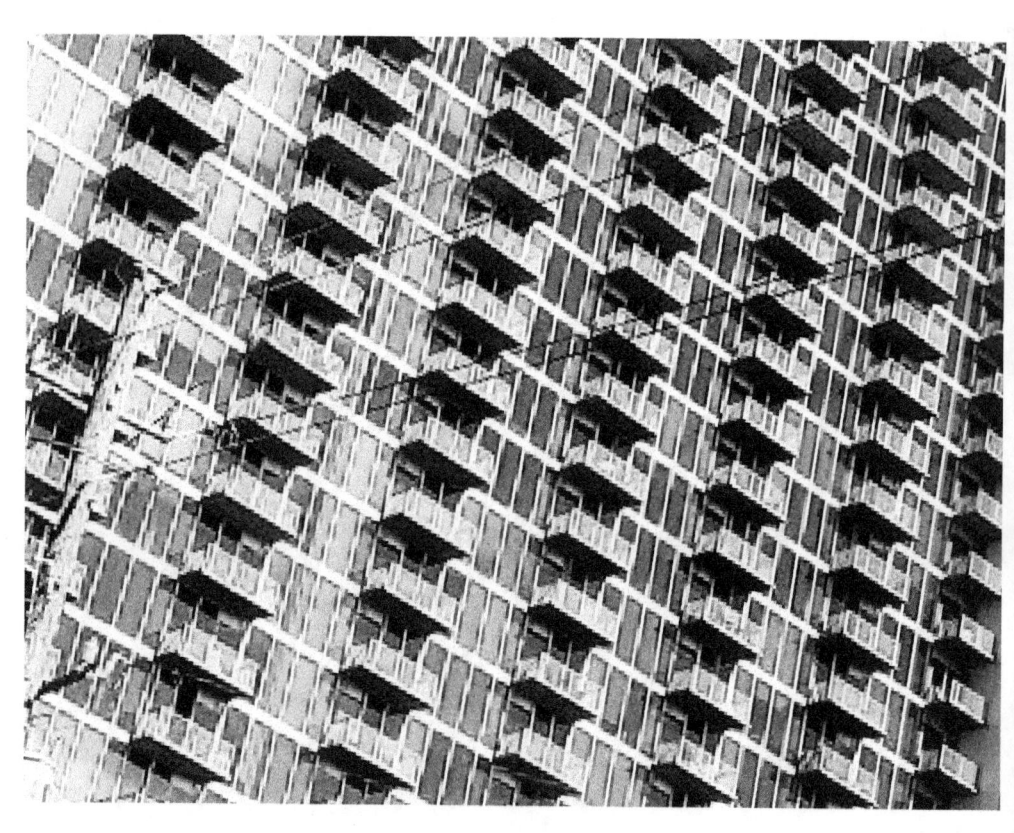

Sideways Architectural Rhythm
February 2015

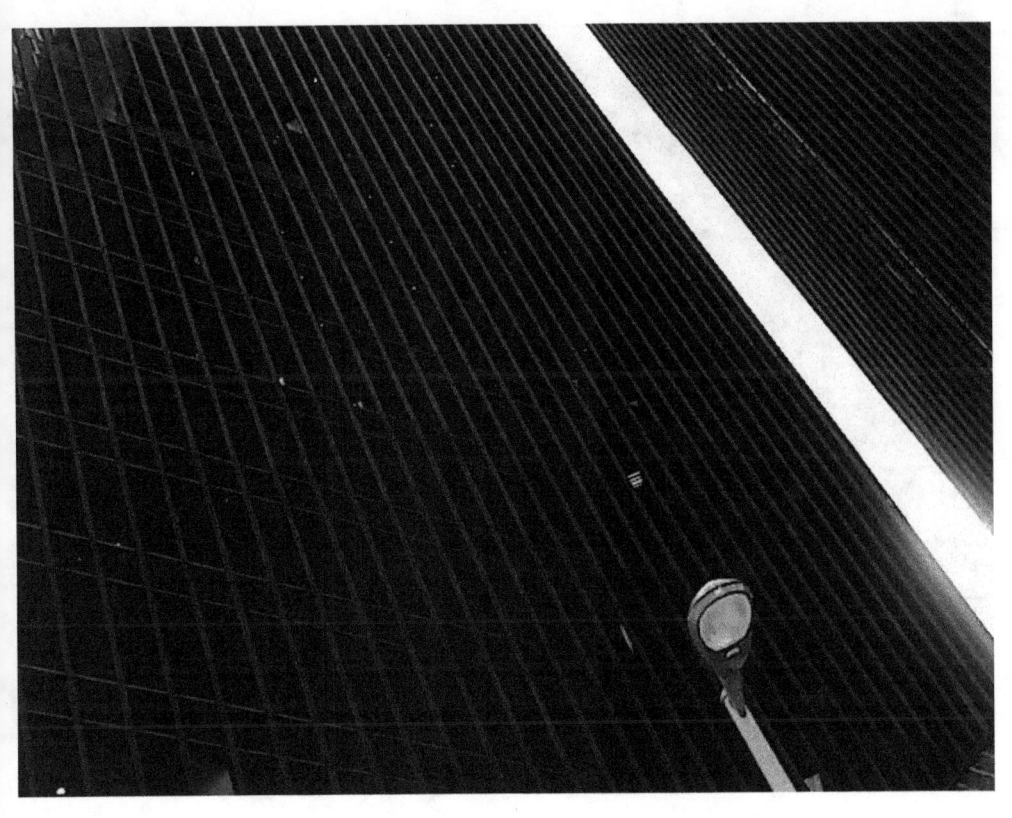

Minimalist Composition, Guilty Pleasure
March 2015

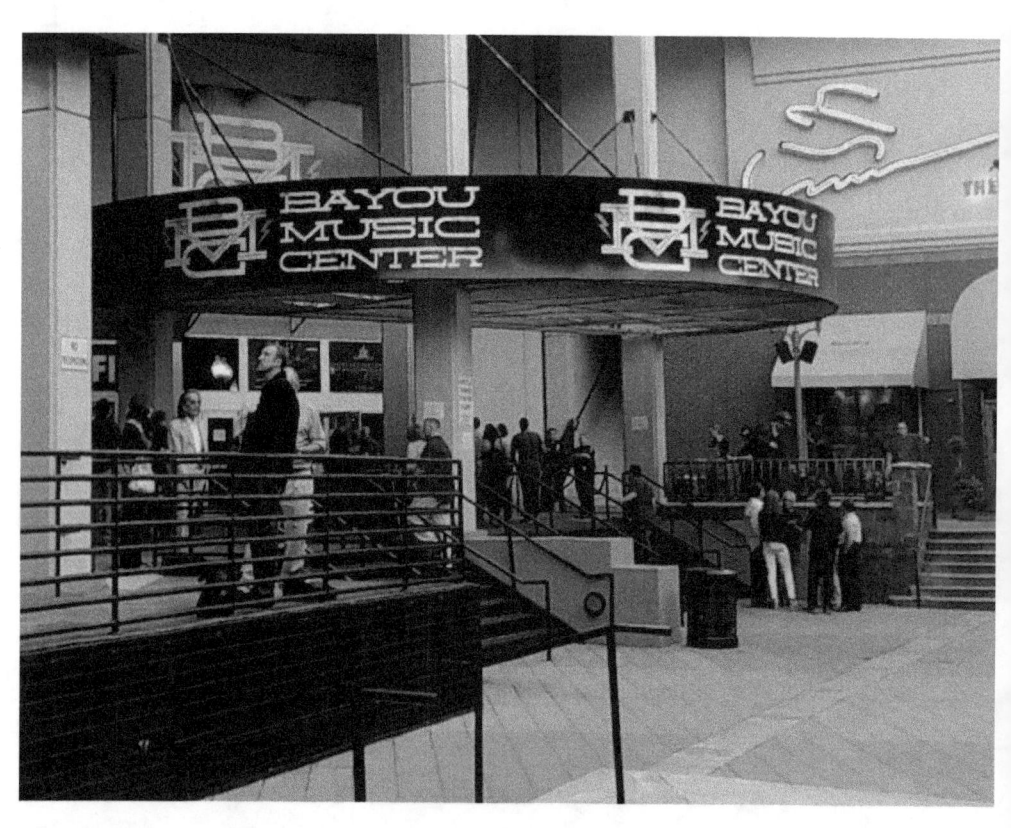

One Hour Before Bob Dylan
May 2015

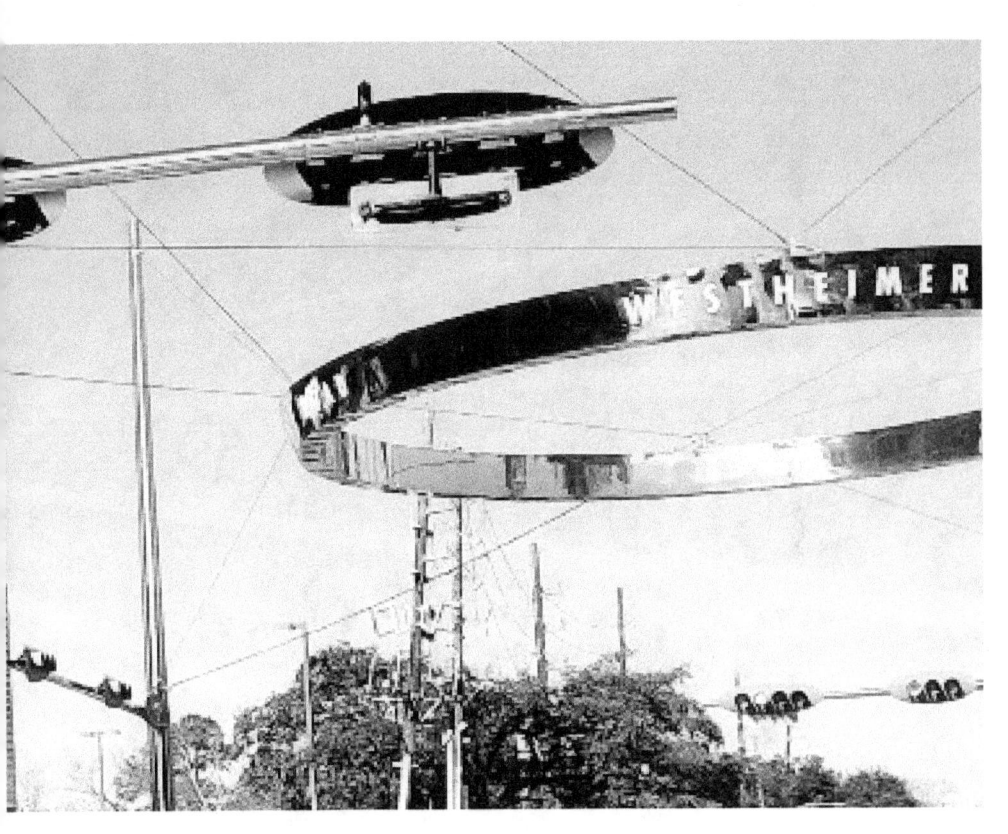

Stuck in Traffic, but Daydreaming Blues
February 2015

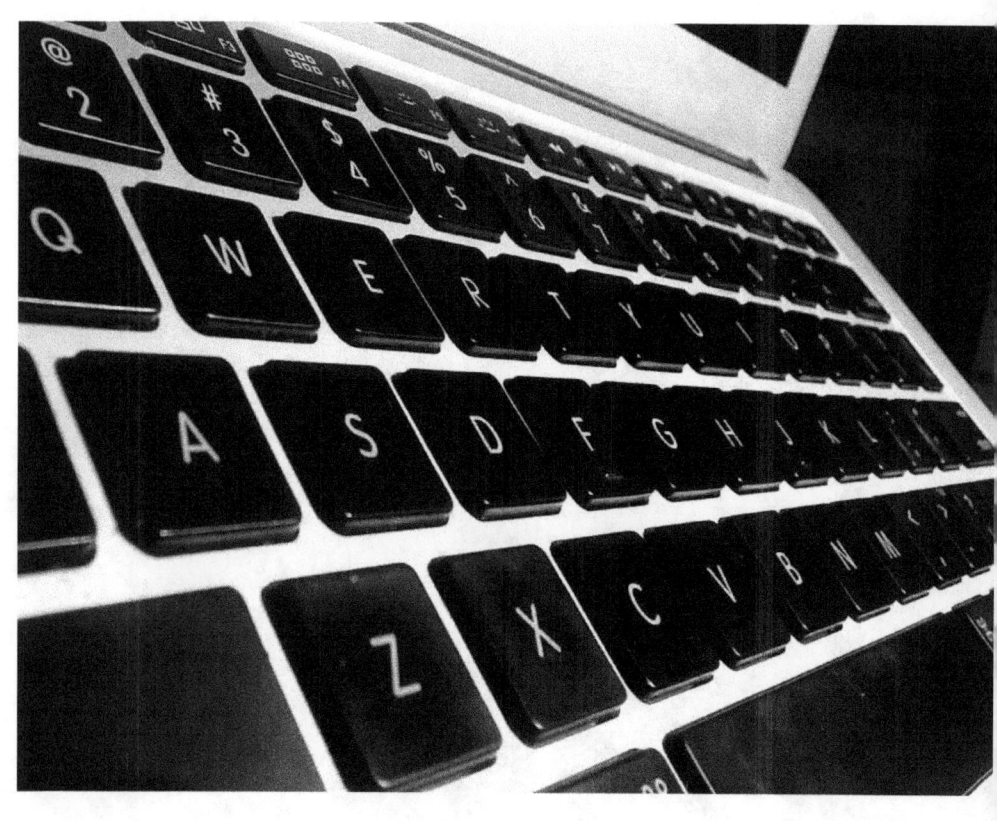

Simply Magic
March 2015

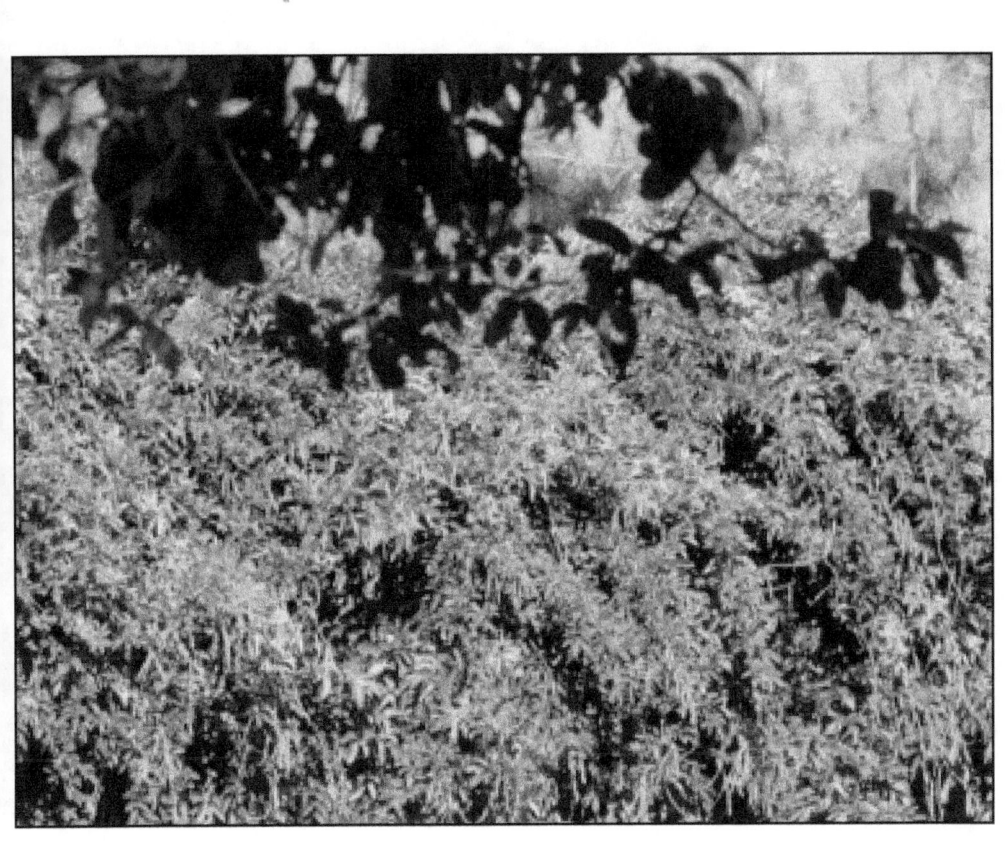

Aesthetics Test
May 2015

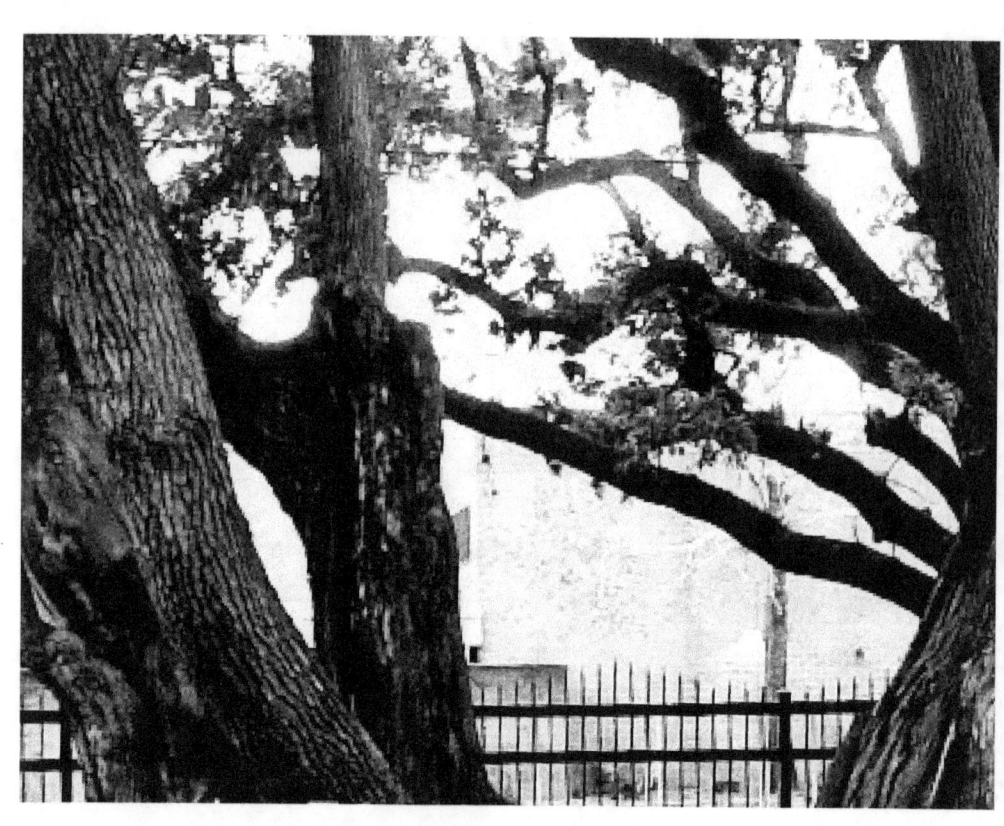

Specializing in Intricate Simplicity
March 2015

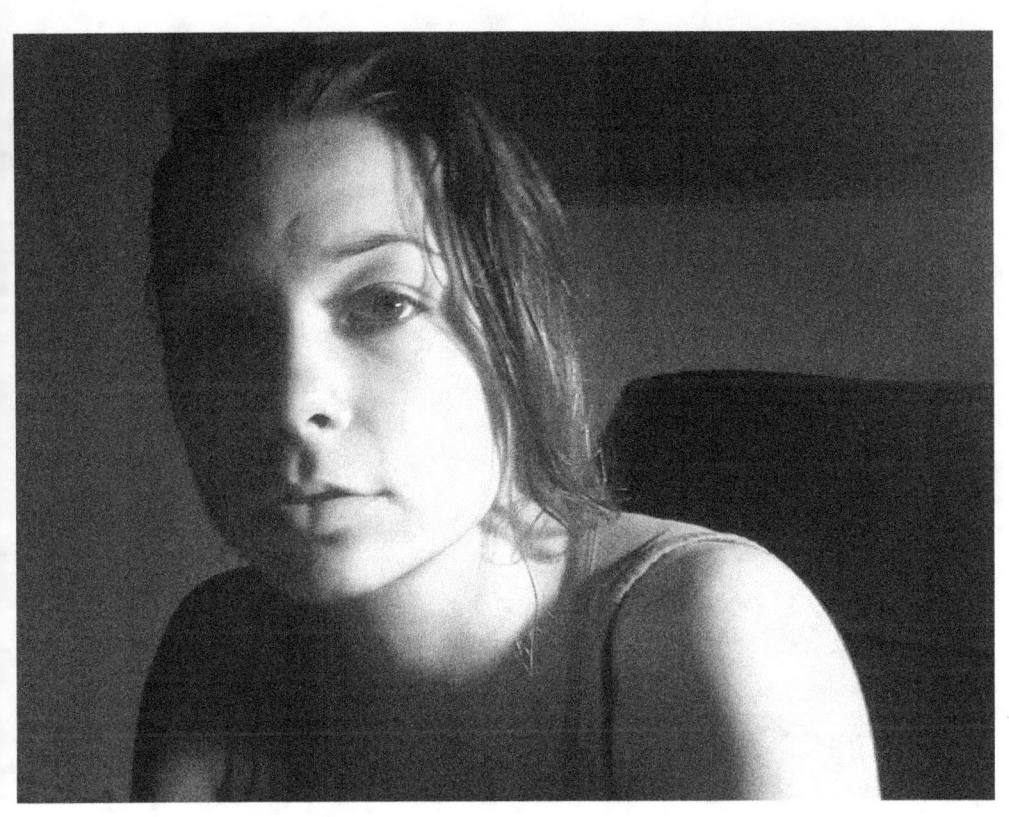

Self-Portrait
May 2015

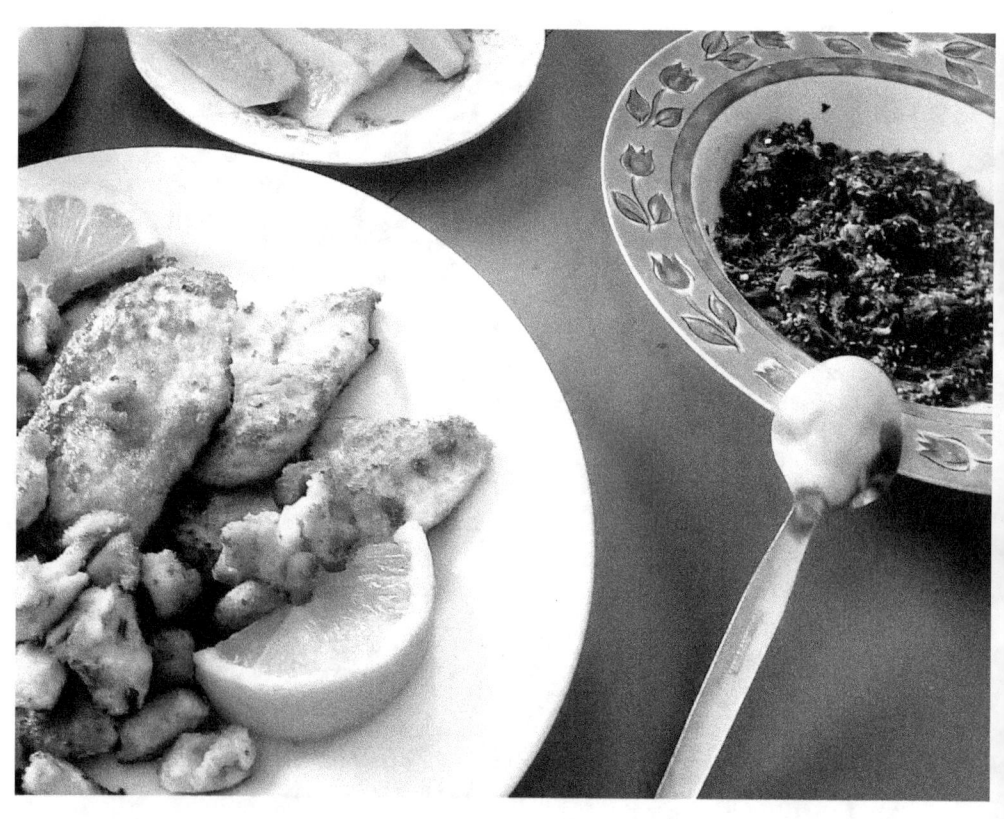

Growth
July 2015

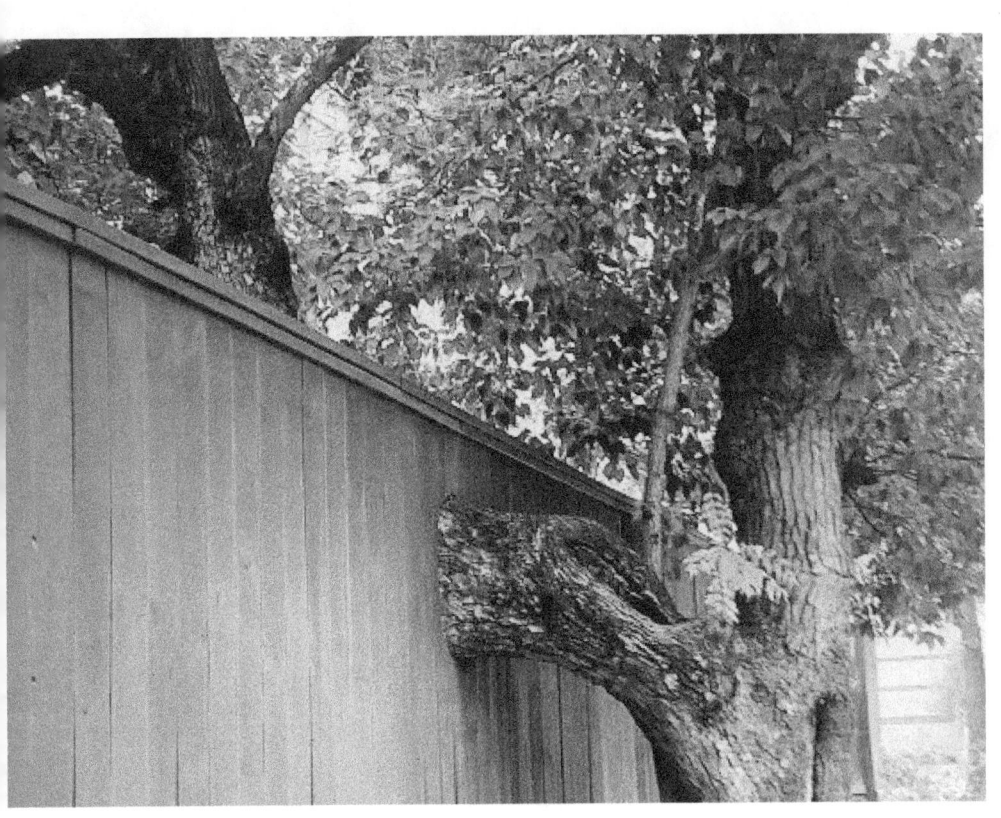

Comical Repression?
November 2014

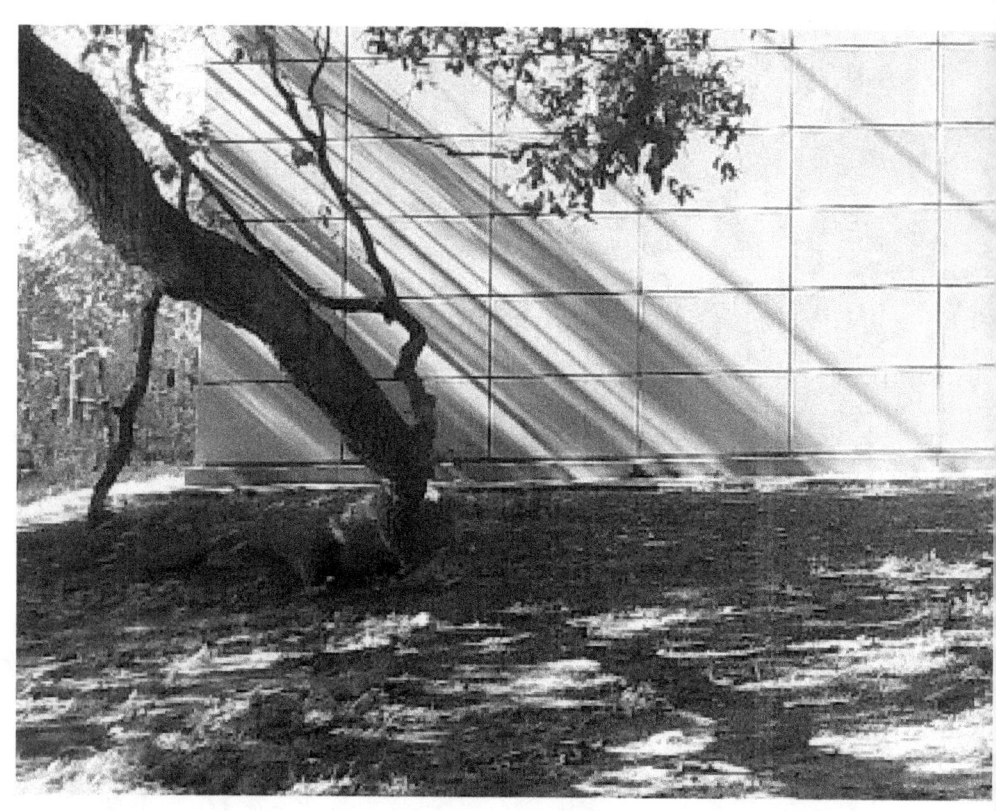

The Blue Jay Way is Solitude
December 2014

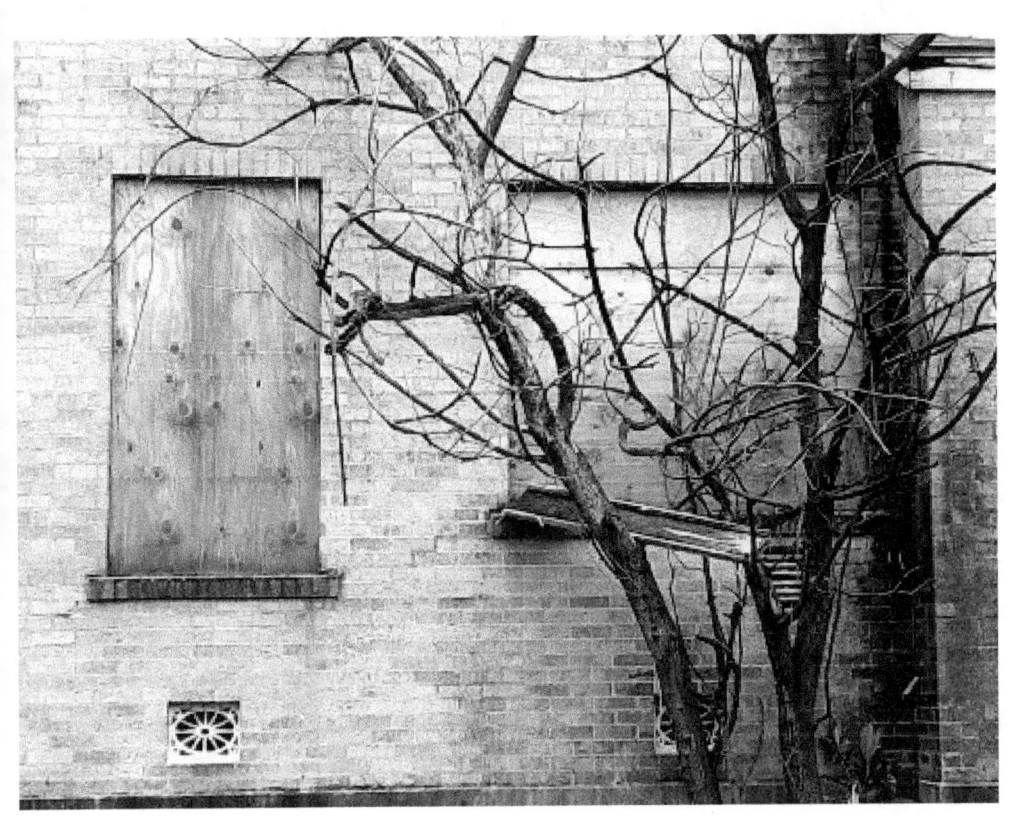

Mutual Attraction for Moments Such as This
January 2015

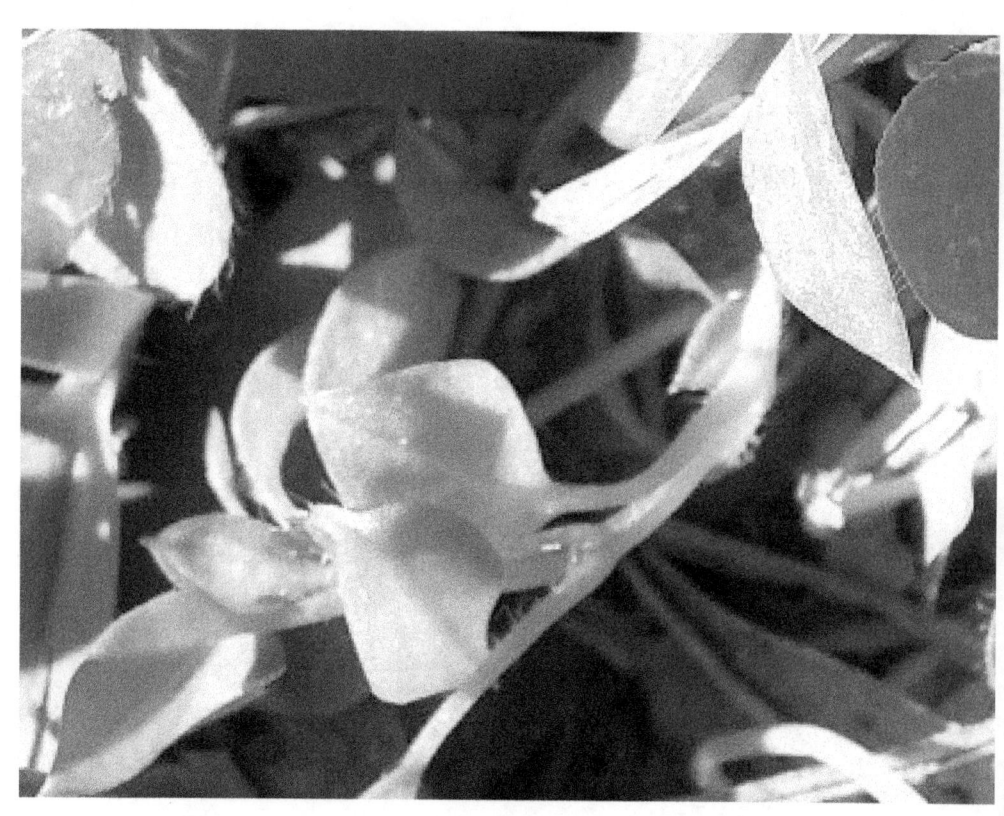

I Will Never Forget
April 2015

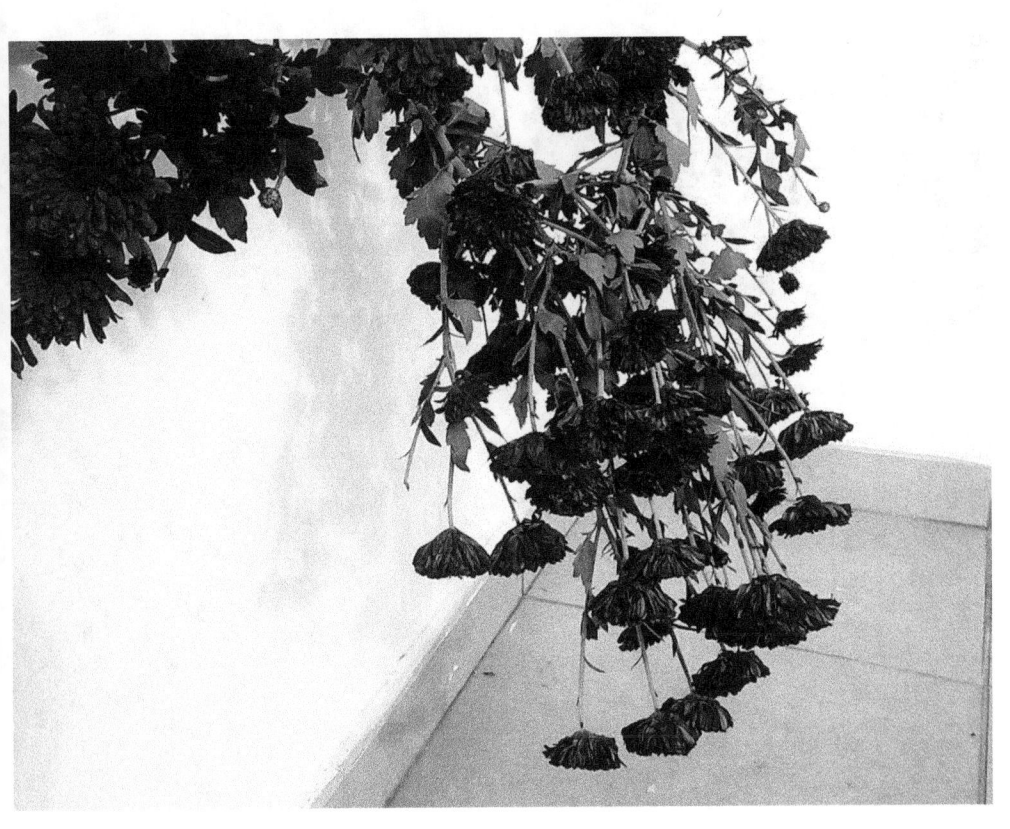

New Love
January 2016

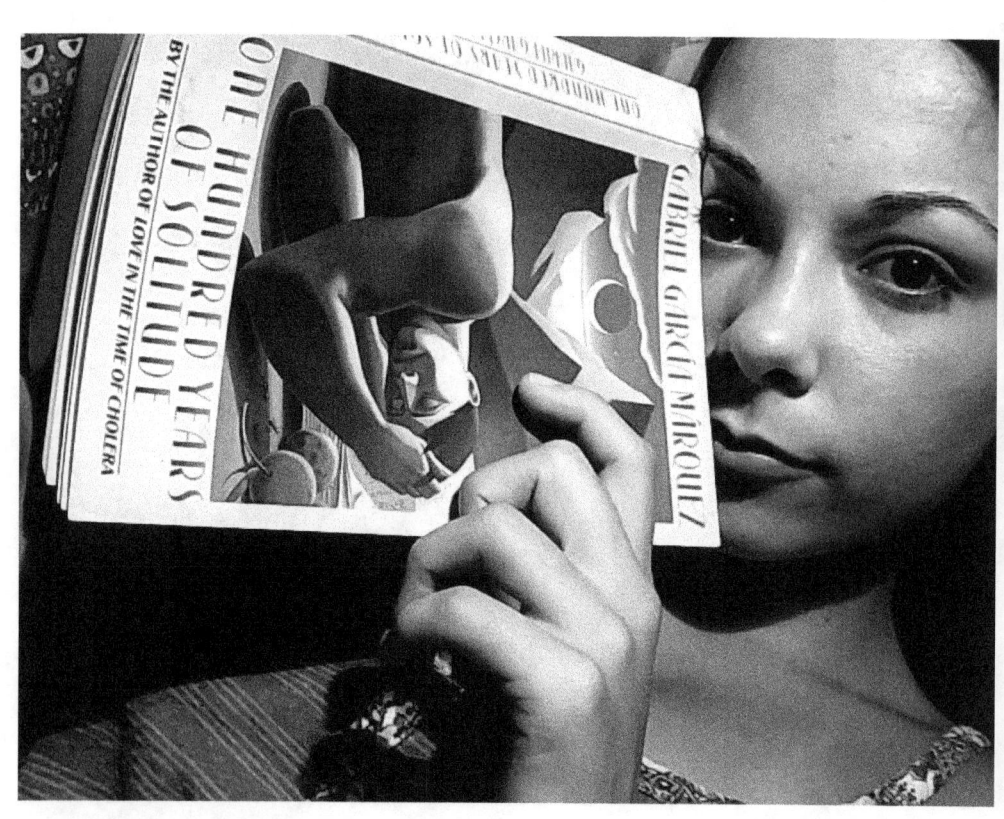

Self-Portrait Con Libro
July 2015

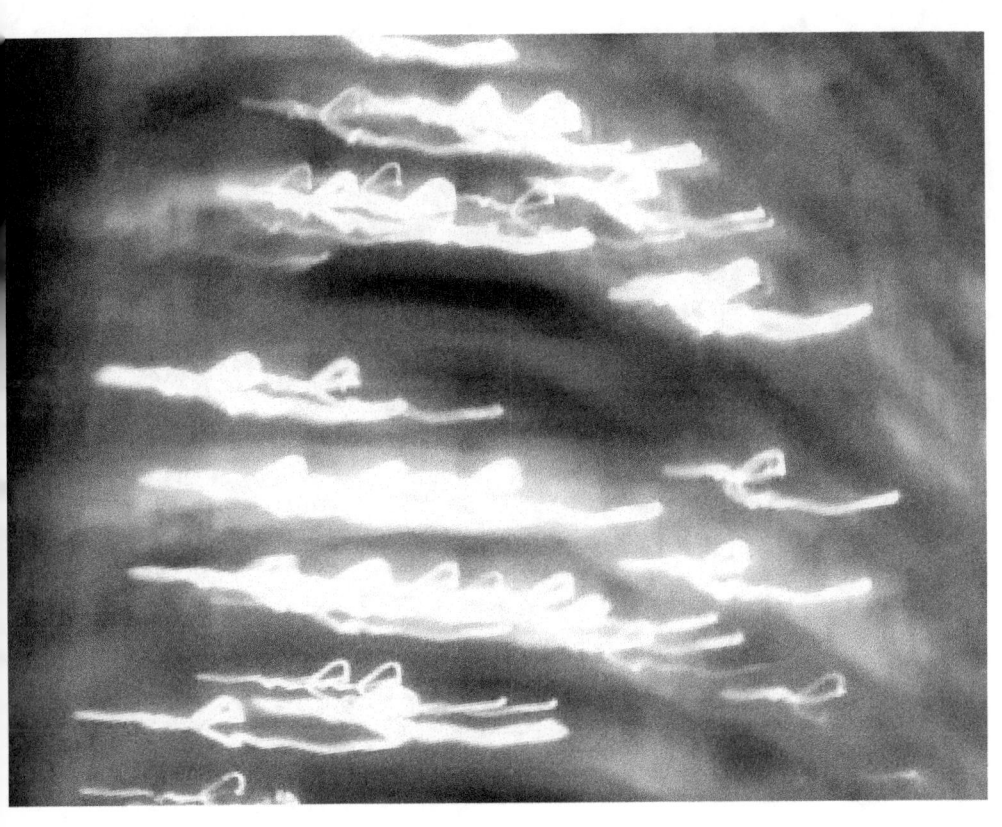

Ticklish Memories Floating, Slightly Impeding
December 2014

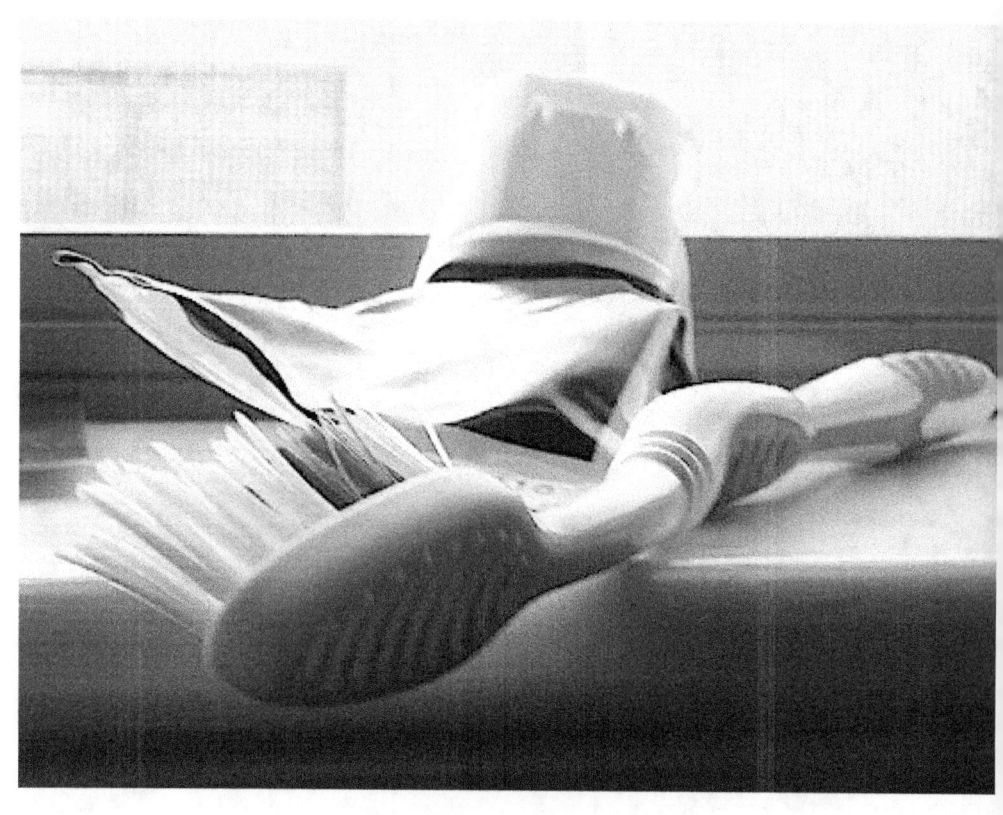

Also, Pack Your Sense of Humour
December 2014

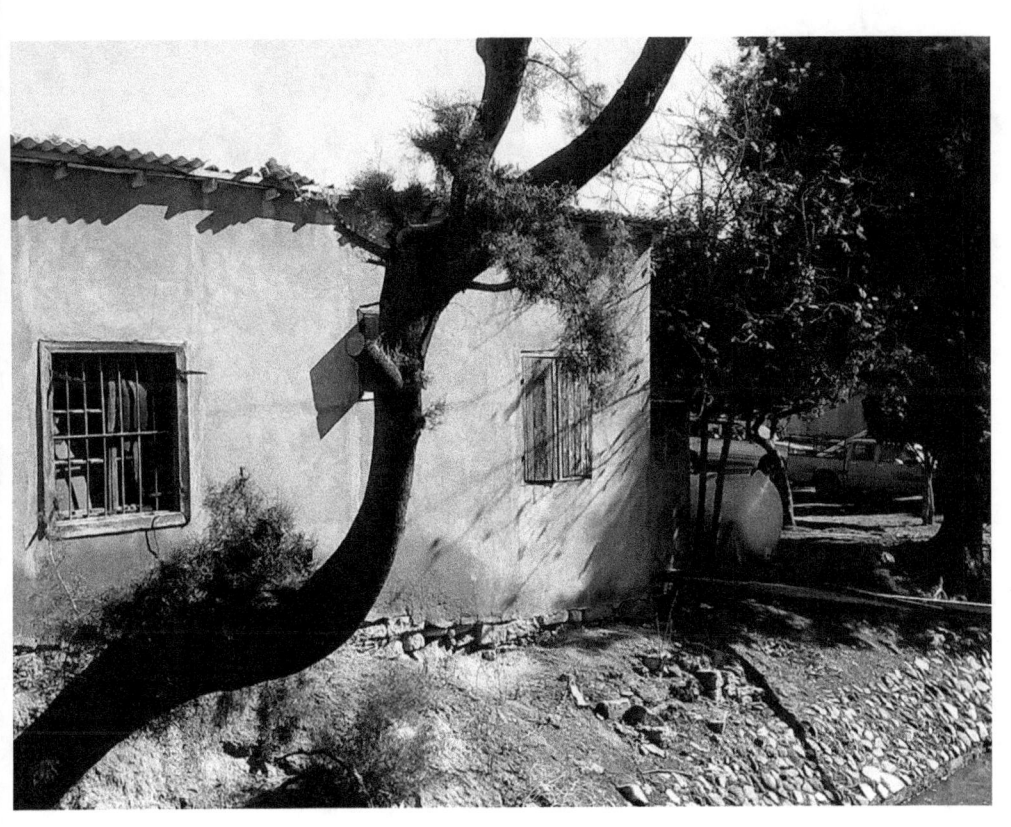

Trespassing by Falling in Love
January 2016

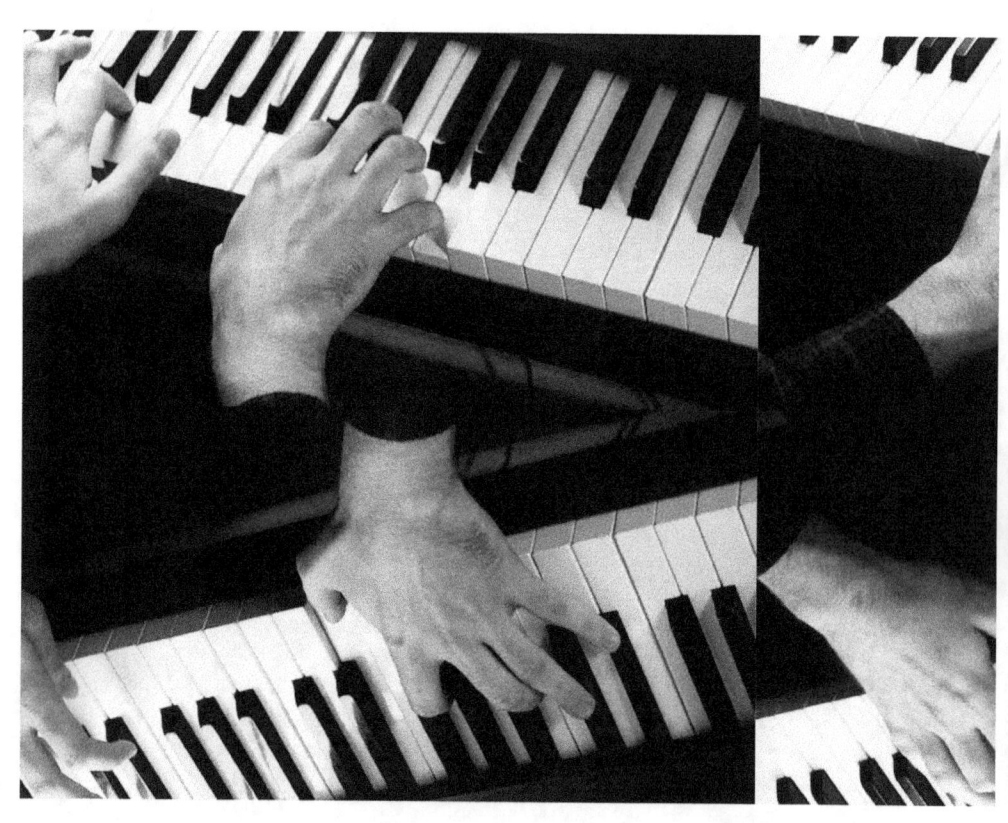

What If? Resonated...
November 2014

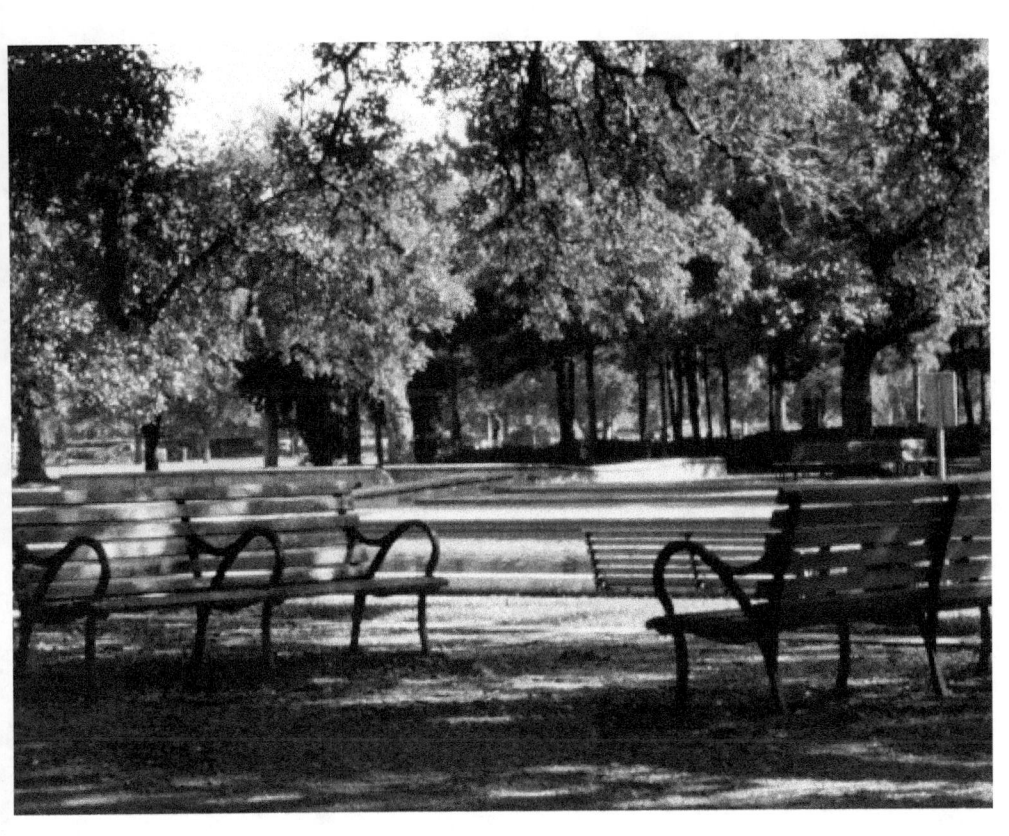

Ghosts
October 2014

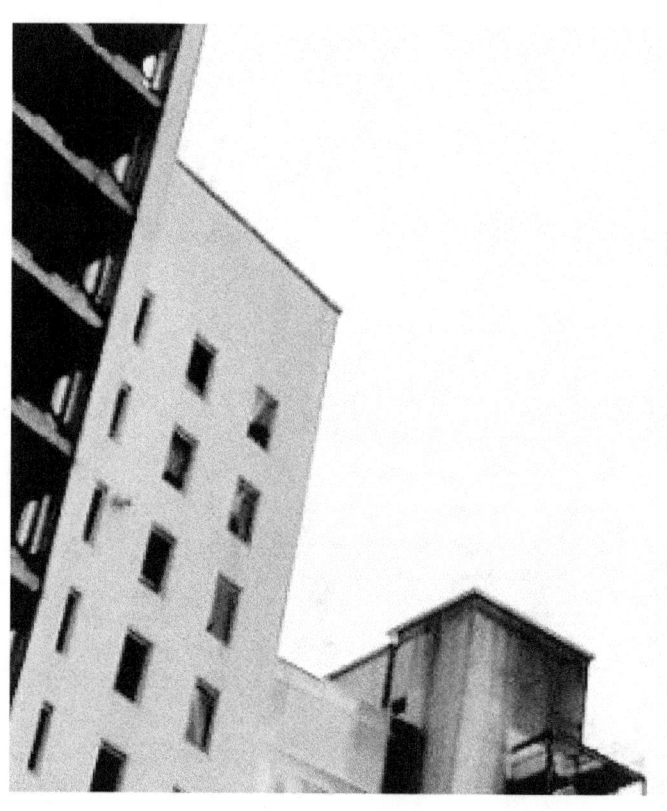

Inexplicable Fascinations (Just Because)
March 2015

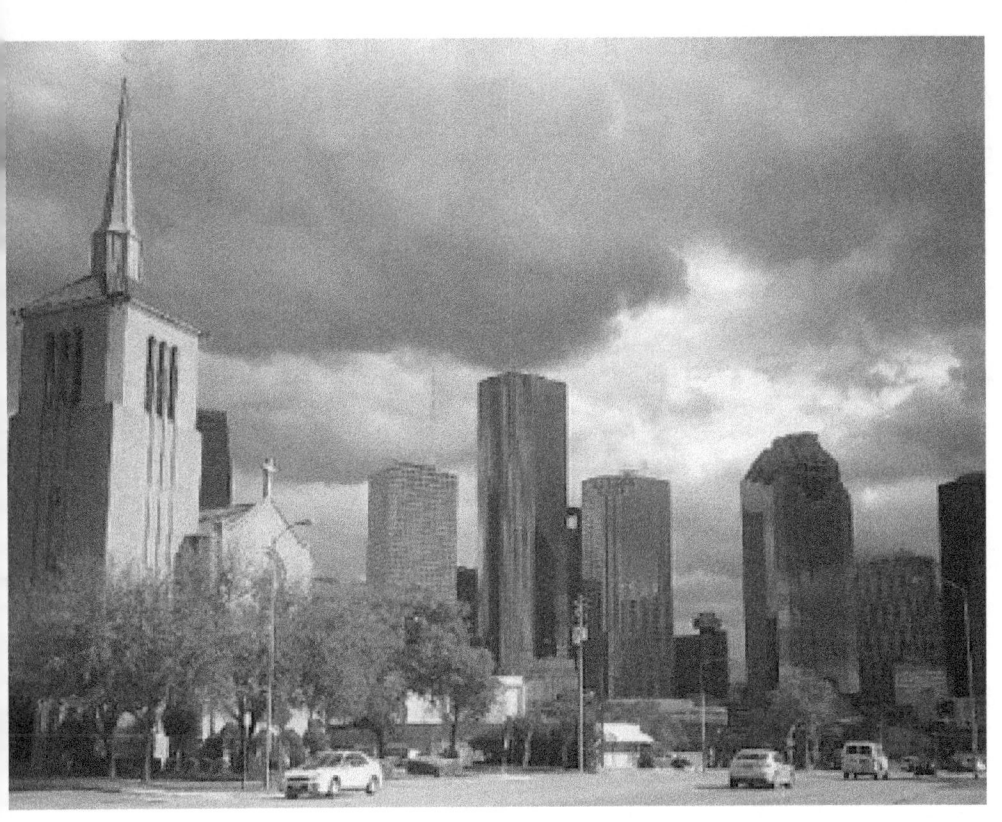

The Long Way Home
April 2015

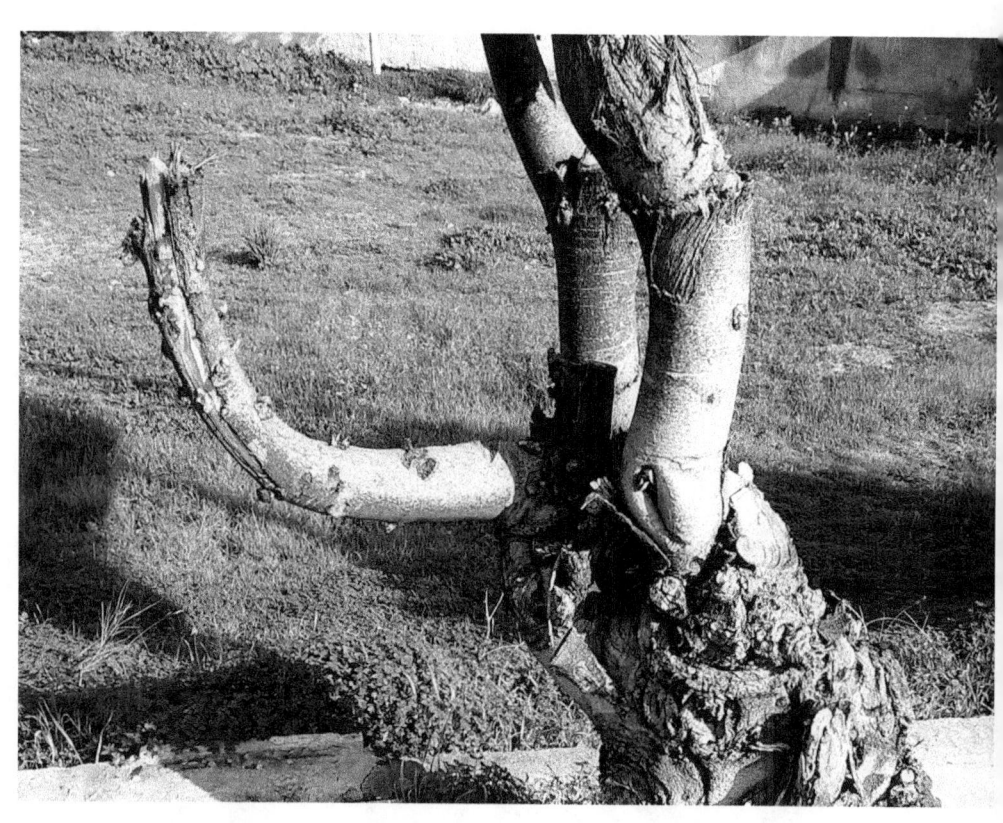

The Biggest Challenge = Starting
January 2016

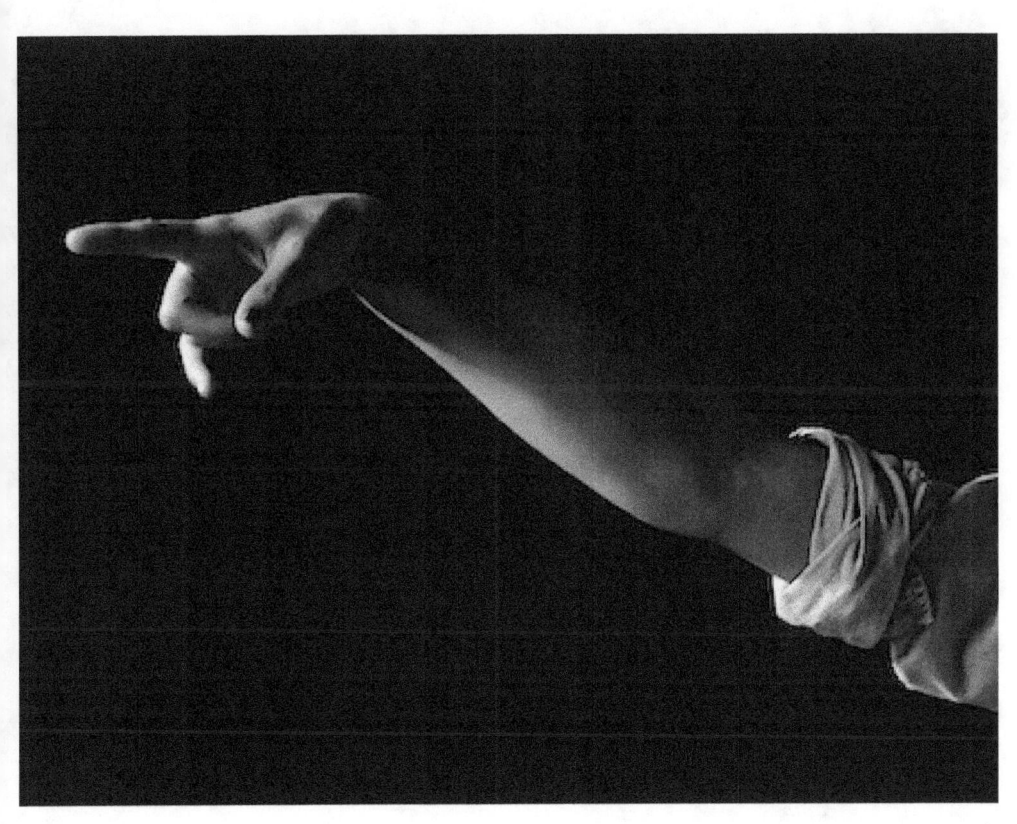

Simply, Go
May 2015

"The More I see
The Less I know
The More I'd Like
To Let It Go"